759.96.

Chinwe Roy

A PROFILE

Verna Wilkins

Tamarind Ltd

OTHER BOOKS IN THE
Black Profiles Series

LORD JOHN TAYLOR OF WARWICK
DR. SAMANTHA TROSS
MALORIE BLACKMAN
BARONESS PATRICIA SCOTLAND
MR JIM BRATHWAITE
BENJAMIN ZEPHANIAH

Visit Chinwe's website at: www.chinwe@chinwe.com

Published by Tamarind Ltd 2002
PO Box 52, Northwood
Middlesex HA6 1UN, UK

Text © Verna Wilkins
Paintings © Chinwe Roy
Cover: Self-portrait in light – oils
Title page: Self-portrait with hat – oil on canvas
Back cover, top left: Verna Wilkins – pastels

ISBN 1-870516-59-1

Printed in Singapore

Contents

For our children
Rhys, Huw, Rogan, Alasdair and Nwiru

and for
Max, Cassidy and Christian

CHAPTER ONE

Dreams

EVEN AS A FIVE YEAR OLD GIRL in Primary School, Chinwe didn't like Maths. She wanted to draw and paint pictures.

"You should try and work a bit harder. Especially with your Maths. Do try," her parents pleaded.

"Work harder or else!" warned her class teacher. So, in Maths lessons, Chinwe put her head down and worked furiously, glancing up at the teacher every minute or two.

Then, one day, his eyes narrowed and he bellowed, "Come here Chinwe. Immediately. Bring your work with you." Chinwe froze.

The teacher strode over to her desk. "What's this?" he shouted, staring at a crazy cartoon of his own head, huge on a shrunken body.

Chinwe ducked under his outstretched arm. She escaped, with the picture, into the hot mid-morning sun, and galloped the full mile home.

"What's wrong?" her worried mother called out to her as she panted into the house.

"The teacher wants to punish me. I couldn't do my Maths."

"He should help you. Not punish you. I'll have a word with him. But, what's that?" Her mother took one look at the picture and her eyes blazed.

Chinwe flew out of the house and ran all the way back to school. For the entire hour of her next Maths lesson, the teacher made her stand on top of her desk. Her humiliation was complete.

Chinwe lost heart and worked her way to the bottom of her class.

At the age of eight, Chinwe moved into a new class. She scampered into the room ahead of everyone and leapt into a seat near a large window. From there, she gazed at street life.

"From my classroom window, I could see sunlight striking the trees. The leaves shone like glass and the stems cast long, dark shadows on the ground. I could see women going to work and to the market in their brightly coloured dresses and head-ties. Buses, trucks and handcarts roared up and down. All this was far more interesting than what was happening inside the classroom, but the teachers called me a dreamer and moved me away from the window. I was sad."

One day, as she walked slowly and miserably across the playground, a kind teacher stopped her. "You're a bright girl. Why won't you do your school work?"

"I want to draw and paint and nobody teaches that," replied Chinwe.

"And where do you think drawing and painting will get you, my girl? You need Mathematics and English, Science and History to succeed in life. Not Art."

Many years later, in the year 2000, far beyond her early dreams, and thousands of kilometres away from her African classroom, Chinwe was chosen to do a portrait of Her Majesty, Queen Elizabeth II, the most prestigious job in the world of portrait painting. Chinwe Roy was the first black person ever to paint the Queen.

Inhambane market
etching

CHAPTER TWO

Early Years

CHINWE WAS BORN IN AWKA, in Eastern Nigeria in Africa. Her mother was a nurse. Her father was a successful businessman. She had three brothers and three sisters. Chinwe was the third child.

Her first school was a large primary school in Awka. She was five years old.

The school day began at 8 o'clock and ended at 2 in the afternoon. It was run by teachers from the Presbyterian Church. They were very strict.

In the classroom, the children were made to sit in neat rows and were harshly disciplined. Even at that early age, they did Maths, English and General Knowledge.

In the playground during break, the girls played a game similar to hopscotch and they loved skipping. The boys played *koso,* a game with a metal cone which they whizzed and spun. Both boys and girls played *okwe*, a popular game with pebbles.

Sometimes, while the other children played, Chinwe found paper and pencils and drew houses, trees and the skinny dogs that slunk around, their tongues hanging loose in the hot sun. She then coloured her pictures at home with wax crayons.

"What are you doing?" her father asked one evening. "This is good. Did you do this by yourself?"

"Yes. But I don't have proper paints to colour with. These wax crayons are so messy."

"I'll see what I can do. Carry on my dear. I've seen some modern art by Picasso. Yours isn't much different!" and he walked away smiling. It was years later before Chinwe heard the name Picasso again and she remembered her father's words.

In the classroom, under the beady eyes of the strict teachers, the pupils all behaved well. However, after school, some boys picked on the girls.

One day, a boy who was particularly horrid followed Chinwe out of school. "Want a fight, arty, crafty, skinny Chinny?" he shouted at her.

The other boys cheered and the chorus started. "Go on... Go on... Get her... Get her..."

Chinwe panicked and tried to escape. But she was very thin and he was huge, and he came thundering at her. In the split second before the clash, Chinwe, like a frightened bird, flung open her arms and flew at him. She locked both arms and both legs fiercely around his bulky body, trapping one of his arms. In desperation, she hung on. He twisted helplessly from side to side, trying to shake her off. She gritted her teeth and clung to him.

"Please let go of me," he groaned.

"Promise not to hit me, then," Chinwe screamed at the top of her voice, right into his ear.

"I won't. Just shut up and let go."

Chinwe loosened her grip and he sloped off down the street, to a chorus of boos and hisses from his friends.

Chinwe gained the respect of her classmates, but she could not wait to leave that school.

CHAPTER THREE

Union Girls

HER NEXT SCHOOL was Union Girls Secondary School in Ibiaku. Chinwe was just eleven years old.

"How far away is my new school?" Chinwe asked her mother.

"Five hours drive from here, but your father and I will try and visit when we can."

Union Secondary was a boarding school. On a large plot of land, there were four buildings which were the classrooms. There were six boarding houses where the pupils lived. Next to the classrooms, there was a chapel and a hall where the entire school met for assembly every day. Nearby, there were separate buildings where the teachers lived.

Although she missed her family and saw them only in the holidays, Chinwe was happy there. She made lots of friends.

The Sports teachers were especially keen for their pupils to do well. Chinwe soon learned that she could escape from double Maths lessons if she was a team leader in sports.

She joined the athletics team and also played netball as often as she could.

Agaba Idu (Masquerade series) – oil on canvas

After two years at Union Secondary School, she was chosen to represent her school in the long jump, high jump and sprinting.

As the champion hundred metre sprinter, she had a group of fans who cheered her on at every sports event.

"Chinwe! Chinwe! GO... GO.... GO...." rang out from the pavilion, as she outstripped all competitors from various schools in the area. She remained a star until a new girl came along and beat her.

"At Union Girls," Chinwe remembers, "our teachers came from various countries. Apart from our Nigerian teachers, we had two teachers from Scotland, one from Ireland and another from England. They were all strict, but kind.

"Why can't we do Art at this school?" Chinwe complained to each one of her teachers.

"Sorry," they replied. "It's not on the curriculum."

Her Science teacher then had a serious talk with her. "Stop complaining, Chinwe. The important subjects you should work on are Science, History, English and Maths. Then there is Latin and French. Art is not that important. Especially for a girl. Most famous artists are men."

Chinwe eventually settled down to work and her

marks gradually improved in all subjects, except Maths.

"At around thirteen or fourteen years of age," Chinwe remembers, "I knew that I had to be an artist no matter what.

"I was in a world of colour, surrounded by the spectacular and colourful Nigerian landscape and brightly coloured fabric, flowers, foliage and fruit.

"There was the elaborately embroidered ceremonial dress for weddings and funerals. Even the ordinary robes worn by the local people made me want to paint. And then there were the Masquerades – a panorama of excitement and movement in vivid colour. If I close my eyes I can still see, after all these years, the masqueraders crowding around the beautiful, intricately-carved front door of my grandfather's house.

"But when the war came and destroyed everything around us, I thought I'd lost my dream."

Union Girls School was proud of its library and kept it well stocked. Chinwe searched the library for Art books and found none. Instead, she discovered the novels of Jane Austen, Charles Dickens and the Brontë sisters, Charlotte and Emily. These books opened up a different world to Chinwe, the world of

African diaspora I – oil on canvas

Ifeoma Ataa (Masquerade series)
oil on canvas

eighteenth and nineteenth-century Britain. They worked wonders for her fertile imagination.

It was not until much later that she found and read Nigerian writers like Chinua Achebe, Cyprian Ekwensi and the poet, Wole Soyinka. Chinwe was inspired by their work and developed an awareness that, as a Nigerian, she too could have a creative and successful future which might influence the world.

Going home to Awka from school for the Christmas holidays was always the best time.

"I belong to the Igbo* people. In Nigeria, there are two hundred and fifty ethnic groups with seventy-three different languages.

"It is our tradition, as Igbos, that we return home to our villages in December. This is the harmattan season, a hot, dry and windy time. At night, the skies are alight with millions of stars. My earliest memories are still clear.

"With the evening meal finished and cleared away, everyone from the houses in the compound gathered in the open space in front of the *Obu*, the building which belongs to the head of the family. We had mats to sit on. It was story time.

"The stories were told by one of my grandfather's wives – a brilliant entertainer. Most of her stories had

* sometimes also spelled Ibo.

a lesson for us children: to be good, to be wise, to be obedient. Some stories were funny and those always had a chorus that we all joined in with. Others were really scary so we huddled close to the adults until we fell asleep. One by one we were carried off to bed.

"It was a wonderful way of life but when the war came, we were separated."

CHAPTER FOUR

Drama

BACK AT SCHOOL, Chinwe joined the Drama Group. Her interest in Drama grew partly from her reading of novels and plays and partly from a burning desire to perform on stage. She loved being in front of an audience.

"Once I was given the most important part in a very serious school play. I played an international lawyer. I was dressed up in an oversized gown and wig, and I strutted around pompously on stage rattling on about my client. I was aware of twittering and giggling in the audience. It was not a funny play.

"What I didn't know was that my wig was skewed and was slowly slipping over my left ear. As I turned and tilted my head at the judge, the wig slipped onto my shoulder. That made me jump.

"It then plopped onto the floor like a dead rabbit. Even the judge couldn't hide her hysterical giggles. I was mortified."

"Going back to my dormitory late that afternoon, I took a short cut that ran alongside the house of the Vice-Principal, Miss Cameron, the teacher from

Scotland. She had a very talkative parrot. Every day, it sat on the porch glaring at passers by.

"In front of the house was an avocado pear tree which bore large delicious fruit. The students were forbidden to pick the fruit.

"As I walked by, I thought of making a sketch of the tree. Then, having checked that no one was around, I picked one of the delicious avocados and ran off.

"Later on, I went back to the house to ask permission to sketch the tree.

"The parrot squawked. 'This one picked a pear…. This one picked a pear… This one…'

"Later, a classmate saw me bent over my exercise book and asked, 'Why are you doing lines in detention?'

"'I was ratted on by a parrot!' I groaned."

Life was good at Union Girls Secondary. Then disaster struck.

CHAPTER FIVE

War

ALL OVER NIGERIA trouble was brewing. There were constant complaints against the government. Some newspapers supported the government while others were against. News on the radio added to people's fears and the situation became extremely serious.

Eventually, on January 15, 1966, there was a military coup. Soldiers from the Nigerian Army attacked and overthrew the government of Prime Minister Tafawa Balewa.

General Ironsi seized power and became leader. He was an Igbo, the ethnic group to which Chinwe's family belonged.

No sooner had Ironsi taken over the government, than rumblings of discontent from the other ethnic groups began. They feared that the new ruler favoured his own people. Rumours of his favouritism spread like wildfire. Many Igbos were attacked and killed.

The Igbo's land was in the south-east, where the oil fields lay. This made their territory rich and self sufficient so the Igbo people decided to 'go it alone' and separate themselves from the rest of Nigeria. Their appointed leader, General Ironsi, declared Igbo independence from the rest of Nigeria. He named their independent state Biafra.

This set off a horrendous conflict and in July, 1967, a full-scale bloody war began.

At Union Girls School, the Head and all the staff made a painful decision.

"Girls, we have called this emergency assembly to tell you that we can no longer be responsible for your safety. The country is at war and we are all in great danger. Please return to your rooms and pack. You are to leave for home immediately. We pray for your safety."

By this time, the war was raging not far from Chinwe's homeland. Many areas had been bombed and the Igbo army was fighting back fiercely.

Chinwe set off on the hazardous journey home to Awka. Transportation was difficult. There were thousands of people travelling in all directions. They passed soldiers in large army vehicles on the way and saw and heard in the distance the fighting planes raining death.

Miraculously, Chinwe made it safely home. Here,

the tension was high but the fighting was still some way off. Gradually, the sounds of war, the bombing and the low flying aircraft drew nearer. Daily news of death and destruction in all the surrounding villages reached them.

Their father was away so Chinwe's mother gathered the children together. "We have to escape. Your father isn't due back from his work for a few days, but we'll all be killed if we don't go now."

"Where will we go?" asked the frightened children. "The war is everywhere."

"Okigwe village. We should be safe with our friends there. Your father will be able to find us."

All along the roads, there was general panic, terrible distress and death. People were fleeing in all directions. Some were desperately searching for their loved ones, some were trying to get home and others were trying to escape, not knowing where to go.

In Okigwe, they were safe for a few weeks, but eventually Chinwe's family took to the dangerous roads again. They became refugees. To make matters worse, Chinwe began to be aware that her parents were not happy with each other any more.

"I cannot bear to say what really happened in that

Dance of the Devils – oil on canvas

terrible, terrible war," says Chinwe. "It's a period of my life that I hate. Even after all this time, I cannot really speak about it.

"I lost my cousin and my best friend Nwabulachi. She was killed when her village was destroyed. Most of our homes and businesses were bombed. Food was scarce.

"A few brave women set up market stalls with whatever foodstuffs they could find. The bombings had flattened their buildings so the surviving market women set up their stalls under the cover of the largest trees left standing. We would rush around their food stalls as fast as we were able, buy as much food as we could carry and dash back to the house," remembers Chinwe.

"The high-speed, low flying aircraft sometimes discovered the stalls under the trees and bombed them.

"When the bombs rained down, everyone ran, everywhere. There was nowhere to hide. Nowhere was safe. Death was everywhere."

When there was no food left and starvation set in, Chinwe's mother made dangerous trips into the fields to feed the family. She dug up roots, picked berries and cooked them.

"That's rubbish," jibed the people around. "You can't eat that!"

But Chinwe's family were the best fed people in the area and they did not starve.

The war raged on and after three years and a million deaths, the Biafran army was utterly defeated. It was devastating, but worse was to follow.

CHAPTER SIX

Severe Illness

SURROUNDED BY FEAR and sadness, Chinwe
was suddenly struck down by a terrible illness. To
make matters worse, her parents separated.

"No one expected me to live. I grew thinner, unable
to walk or talk. Friends came to visit thinking that it
would be the last time they would see me alive.

"I was dangerously ill for two years. I couldn't
stand to see the worry in my mother's face.

"None of the local doctors knew what was wrong.
They'd never seen patients with my symptoms. They
were puzzled. They couldn't help."

Then one day a new doctor arrived in the village.
He diagnosed Chinwe's illness as myasthenia gravis, a
serious disease. He gave Chinwe an injection and
after only thirty minutes she stood up.

"The series of injections that followed seemed
miraculous."

Myasthenia gravis is a disease which attacks the
muscles, slowly weakening them. The disease can
affect the muscles of the eyes and face, making it
difficult for sufferers to chew, talk, swallow or even

breathe. People with myasthenia may have difficulty walking or moving their legs, arms and neck.

If you are healthy and you want to move a leg, for example, your brain sends a message through the nervous system to that leg telling it what to do. The message is carried by special chemicals made by the body. In people suffering from myasthenia gravis, the body's own antibodies – special chemicals whose job is to fight off disease – attack these normal chemical transmitters thinking they are dangerous illnesses that are trying to harm the body. The message doesn't get through to the muscles which, over time and due to lack of proper use, become weak and stop working properly.

Myasthenia gravis can be controlled by treatment and most patients can expect to lead normal lives.

When Chinwe recovered and was well enough to start back at school, her mother wasn't happy to send her back to a school far away from home.

She enrolled her in the nearest school, which was Igwebuike Grammar School – an all boys' school.

"Do I have to go there?" Chinwe complained. "The boys will tease me." And of course, they did.

"Hey! Now that she's here, we won't be bottom of the class," jibed the idlers.

Chinwe made them eat their words. She steadily worked her way to the top of the class.

"You've done well! You've passed nearly all your examinations. You should go into further education," advised her teachers.

Chinwe was excited. "Now I can do what I really want to do. Art."

"You might have a problem there," her teachers warned. "You might have to travel. Because of the war, the waiting lists to get into university are long. Moreover not many of the colleges and universities here in Nigeria have Art on the syllabus."

But Chinwe was hopeful. Her mother was solidly supportive and, although still concerned about her health, was happy for her to travel across the world.

CHAPTER SEVEN

England

CHINWE APPLIED TO COLLEGES in England, where there was a wide selection of courses in Art.

"I was so excited. For me it was a marvellous adventure. But I was sad to leave my mother, brothers and sisters. We had grown very close during the war and during my long illness."

In 1975, on a very cold winter morning, Chinwe arrived in England. At last, she could study Art.

She eagerly attended her first class at East Ham College in London. Here, she could do all the subjects which she needed for a Degree in Art.

The College library contained a whole section on Art. There were dozens of Art books with drawings, paintings and sculptures from all over the world, dating from medieval to modern times.

"I found books on the work of Picasso. I remembered that when I was a little girl, my father had said that my first drawing and painting was not much different from his. I was fascinated and delighted to read that Picasso was influenced by African art. He had been introduced to African sculpture by Matisse, another very famous painter. Both artists had been major influences in revolutionising Western Art. My confidence grew daily."

Inside College and at home, in her uncle's house, in East London, Chinwe kept snug and warm. Going to and from College made her cold to her bones.

Although the vast majority of her early reading books in Nigeria were from England and about life in England, and her Christmas carols and cards were about snow, nothing prepared Chinwe for the real thing.

"Snow is very romantic when you read about it in Nigeria. It's very different walking on grey-brown slush, frozen rigid, teeth chattering and fingers and toes curved numb," she remembers with a shudder.

At first, it seemed that life in England was almost the exact opposite to life in Nigeria.

"The people, the food, the language and especially the weather were so very strange.

"I had to get used to wearing heavy winter clothes. My feet felt leaden in boots. My hands were awkward in gloves. Even inside thick mittens, my fingers were frozen stiff.

"For the first half hour in college, I would have to

warm my hands with my breath before I could hold a pencil.

"I longed for Awka. For the warmth and the hustle and bustle of life in the village with my large extended family. It was almost a year before I really settled down."

Despite the discomfort and homesickness, Chinwe grew used to life in England. She wanted to learn about every aspect of Art and spent hours in the library studying Art History and reading about the lives of the artists.

She visited art galleries on her own and with her group from College. She experimented with strong, vivid colours of ochre, brown, blue and gold for her paintings of the African landscape. She would contrast this by using the paler greens, greys and blues for the wintry Scottish landscapes.

Life couldn't get much better.

CHAPTER EIGHT

Romance

AFTER HER FOUNDATION COURSE at East Ham College, Chinwe applied and was accepted to do a degree in Graphic Design at Hornsey College in North London.

To earn extra money while she was a student, Chinwe worked as an assistant in a petrol station. It was here that she met her future husband.

One day, she looked up in response to the voice of a tall, handsome man saying something to her. He was paying for his petrol and speaking, she thought, an unfamiliar language.

"Pardon me! I don't understand," she answered in English. He looked horribly embarrassed.

"I was saying 'thank you' in Igbo!" he explained.

"*Dalu* is thank you," said Chinwe, smiling.

"*Dalu,*" he repeated with a grin.

"How did you know exactly where I come from?" Chinwe asked.

"I've been working in Nigeria. I knew you weren't from the Hausa, Yoruba or Edo group, so I guessed Igbo, and I was right."

Chinwe gave him his change and he left the petrol

station. She was sure she would never see him again. But to her delight he returned the following week, and from then on, stopped at the petrol station regularly.

"Eventually, he asked me for a date," says Chinwe – that was the start of a relationship that led to marriage in 1980. In 1981 their first son was born and a second son was born five years later in 1986.

The family settled in Lightwater, Surrey, to raise their two young sons. Chinwe practised her painting by doing portraits of the boys.

The children attended the local playgroup. At a birthday party at their home, a visitor saw some of Chinwe's work. "This is fantastic, Chinwe, this painting of your boys."

"Thank you," said Chinwe. "Would you like me to do a portrait of your daughter?"

"Would you? Would you really?" The woman was delighted.

Word spread around the playgroup and soon Chinwe was asked to do many of the little boys and girls.

"Sometimes it was really difficult. Little ones do not like to sit still. I learned quite a lot painting those active children."

Mademoiselle Melanie Dancell
oils

CHAPTER NINE

Family Life

IN 1990, CHINWE AND HER FAMILY moved to Suffolk to take care of her ageing parents-in-law who lived in a beautiful part of the English countryside.

The house is an extended mill cottage, built across the River Deben. The original, old part of the house was built in the eleventh century and is mentioned in the Domesday Book.

Chinwe can put her brushes away and sit at the door of her studio, to watch white swans glide gracefully up and down the river.

In Suffolk, Chinwe joined various Art groups and began painting landscape and still life. She also did sculpting in clay.

Her studio is packed with a magnificent selection of her work. Her paintings vary widely, from the fiercely political (see *Dance of the Devils* on p. 21, where she shows two greedy men exploiting her country's wealth) to tender, loving family portraits and self portraits.

Tragically, in 1995, Chinwe's father fell ill and died.

She returned to Nigeria for the funeral. Her father was an Ozo man which means that he was a highly respected member of his group. The funeral was very grand. The various ceremonies to honour him lasted nearly a whole month.

Chinwe was inspired by one particular ceremony where robed Ozo men announce the death of a brother. They travel through the night blowing horns to tell the world that one of them has died. They return to the village at dawn.

On her return to England, Chinwe worked successfully on a series of paintings based on the funeral.

CHAPTER TEN

Flying High

PAINTING IS THE FOCUS of Chinwe's life. However, she has a keen interest in sport. She follows her favourite football team, Arsenal, and also supports Ipswich. She cheers them on enthusiastically at every match from her sofa.

To her delight, in 1996, she was introduced to Kriss Akabusi MBE, the athlete and Olympic medallist. Chinwe painted his portrait.

He was so delighted with her work that he commissioned six large paintings for his country mansion. The theme of the paintings is the slave trade. They show Africans free in their own land (*African diaspora I*, page 12), then being captured, taken into slavery and shipped in chains to strange lands. The colours are strikingly vivid and capture the heat of the African landscape, the comfort of life in the village and the pain of slavery. The final picture in this series is full of hope and celebration (*African diaspora V*, page 41).

Chinwe's work was becoming well known and she was honoured at the 1997 Women of the Year Lunch

Ndo Ozo 1 (Procession at dawn)
oil on canvas

Kriss Akabusi MBE
pastels
37

at London's Savoy Hotel. There she met many famous black people, such as Floella Benjamin, who works in children's television, Moira Stuart, BBC news presenter, Brenda Emmanus, another television presenter, and Tessa Sanderson MBE, the Olympic gold medallist javelin thrower.

"It was wonderful to be in the company of all these people whom I had seen only on television. I cannot remember what we had to eat, but I remember the people. I had a great time," says Chinwe.

In 2000, Chinwe was asked to paint the portrait of His Excellency Chief Emeka Anyaoku, the Secretary General of the Commonwealth – and she produced a masterpiece.

It was unveiled by Her Majesty, the Queen. Chinwe's family attended the function and they all met the Queen. That portrait now hangs in Marlborough House, London.

"When His Excellency Chief Emeka Anyaoku suggested that I submit my portfolio in a bid to do Her Majesty's portrait, I was overjoyed and quite nervous. And then I was chosen to paint the Queen! I was absolutely thrilled to have this honour."

CHAPTER 11

The Peak of Her Career

IN THE MIDST of all the excitement, and with Chinwe nearly at the peak of her career, another tragedy struck her family.

Her younger sister died in Nigeria in childbirth. The baby girl survived.

Devastated, Chinwe flew immediately to Nigeria. She adopted her niece, who has now completed her family in Suffolk.

Chinwe returned to England in April 2001, just one week before she was due to go to Buckingham Palace.

With the new baby to care for, she didn't have much time to focus on the forthcoming visits to the Palace. "On my first visit I was very nervous," she remembers. "The wide, sweeping drive into the palace grounds is impressive and the enormous rooms are very grand indeed.

"There are dozens of portraits of important people in some rooms, all done by famous artists. I was almost overwhelmed.

"The Queen entered and greeted me with a warm smile and a handshake and I felt more relaxed. I

H.E. Chief Emeka Anyaoku TC GCVO CON
Secretary General of the Commonwealth
oil on canvas

African diaspora V – oil on canvas

addressed her as 'Your Majesty' and did a very wobbly curtsey. After a while, I started to call her Ma'am because everyone else did.

"She remembered me from the unveiling of my portrait of Chief Emeka Anyaoku the year before. I was delighted.

"She also mentioned that many years ago, a Nigerian artist had done a sculpture of her. She could not recall his name. I reminded her that it was Ben Enwonwu. From that moment, I was totally at ease.

"The Queen is a wonderful person to work with. She asked about my family here and in Nigeria. I told her about the baby and how good my sons were becoming at childcare.

"She talked about her family as well. She is humorous and has a keen eye for detail."

"In all, I was allowed five sittings and was given permission to take photographs of her. I brought out my bright new shiny digital camera and snapped away at all angles.

"She sat and watched and then asked about the camera. I explained how images could be fed into my computer and emailed to any chosen destination worldwide. She seemed very impressed and sat comfortably while I did my first few sketches."

"On my third visit, I asked if I could take some more photographs. She agreed and I took out my battered, old camera.

"'Where's that wonderful camera?' asked the Queen.

"I had to admit that none of the pictures from the fancy new camera were any good. We both laughed."

"Her Majesty was extremely generous with her time. Each sitting was due to last for one hour. She usually stayed longer, quite happily.

"However, on the third sitting, she had to leave promptly in order to attend a meeting with the President of the United States of America, President George W. Bush."

"There were times when I had to stop and pinch myself. It seemed almost surreal – here I was, in Buckingham Palace painting a portrait of Her Majesty the Queen – a long way from Awka."

The portrait was commissioned by the Commonwealth Secretariat to mark the Queen's Jubilee and the Commonwealth Games in Manchester in 2002. It will hang between portraits of King George V and Queen Mary at Marlborough House in London.

Her Majesty Queen Elizabeth II – oil on canvas